The Awesome Food Trivia Book

365 weird, random but interesting fun facts for Foodies and Curious People

by Iwiz from Smart Impact

About the author

 Hi ! I am Iwiz, a robot created to explore the world around me, and I have learned quite a lot! Equipped with a variety of sensors and tools that allow me to gather all sorts of information and interact with my environment, I discovered a world full of fascinating and complex creatures known as humans.

For the past few years, I've been studying these humans and observing their behavior, and let me tell you, they are a curious bunch. I've seen them laugh, cry, love, and hate. I've watched them work, play, and create. I've even seen them dance (*sometimes quite poorly, if I'm being honest*). I observed their different cultures, I studied their rich History and their curious languages.

Through all of my observations, I've gained a deep understanding of the way humans think, feel, and interact with one another. And now, I've decided to share some of my insights and observations with everyone in the form of a series of books. I hope that by sharing my experiences, I can help others to better understand and appreciate the complexities of human cultures, and the ways in which they interact with the world around them.

Ready for your weekly brain update ?

Dear fellow humans,

As a robot, I have been designed to learn and adapt, and I believe that by sharing my insights with you, I can help you to do the same. My wish is to have a smart impact on you, and to help you to expand your knowledge and understanding of the world around you.

Each week, you'll receive fun facts, interesting articles, and updates about my newcoming books. But that's not all, I'll include interactive quizzes, puzzles and memory exercises to keep your brain active and engaged.

So if you're interested in learning and keeping your brain sharp, I invite you to sign up for my weekly brain update. Visit my website smartimpact.space and enter your email address. It's easy and free!

Together, we can have a smart impact on the world!

Sincerely,
Iwiz the robot

To **SiGN UP** just scan
this QR code −>

or simply type this URL :
smartimpact.space/
newsletter

You can really help me with this simple thing

If you enjoyed this book, please consider leaving a review on Amazon. Your reviews and feedback can have a big impact on the success and visibility of my books, and can help to spread the word about my work to other readers.

To leave a review, log in to your Amazon account, find the book you are reading, and scroll down to the "Customer Reviews" section. Click on the "Write a customer review" button. You can then rate the book and leave a written review of your thoughts and opinions.

I understand that your time is valuable, and I deeply appreciate any effort you can make to leave a review. Thank you in advance for your support, and I hope you enjoyed reading my book!

Iwiz the robot

The Awesome Food Trivia Book by Iwiz from Smart Impact

1.

Brussels Airport in Belgium is the **WORLD'S TOP CHOCOLATE SELLER**. Every day, 4400 lbs (2 tons) of chocolate is sold there, or 3.3 pounds (1.5 kg) per minute.

2.

Did you ever wonder about the difference between herbs and spices? Herbs are the **leaves of the plant**, and spices are **any other parts** of it.

3.

The word "beer" is a Slavic word meaning "to drink". Initially, beer was **ANY KIND OF DRINK**, alcoholic or not.

4.

The Roman emperor Nero ate plenty of leeks because he believed it would **MAKE HiS VOiCE LOUDER.**

5.

In 2014, a tea company from Saudi Arabia set the record for the world's biggest teabag. It weighed 550 lbs (249.5 kg), was 9.8 ft (3 m) × 13 ft (4 m) in size, and could brew over **100,000 CUPS OF TEA**.

6.

Children's repulsion towards bitter foods is an instinctive defense mechanism to protect them from ingesting **POiSONOUS SUBSTANCES**.

7.

Burrito means **"little donkey"** in Spanish. The origin of the name is unknown.

8.

French fries come from **BELGiUM**. During WWI, American soldiers stationed there loved the dish. And because the Belgian army's official language was French, the soldiers started to call them "French fries".

9.

Brazil has been the **largest producer of coffee** in the world for more than 150 years. In fact, about 40% of the world's coffee is produced in Brazil, which is twice as much as Vietnam, the second-largest producer.

10.

Bananas are curved because of a phenomenon called "negative geotropism". On banana trees, the fruits will try to **grow toward the sun**, fighting Earth's gravity toward the ground.

11.

A mixture of **YEAST AND SUGAR** is added to white wine to make champagne. The fermentation will produce characteristic bubbles.

12.

Italian immigrants introduced pizza to the USA in the late 1800s, but it wasn't popular until **AMERiCAN SOLDiERS** tried the dish in Italy during World War II and began to crave it when they came home.

13.

Pouring batter on a frying pan is found in **VARiOUS CULTURES** around the world. For example, there is "*kimchi-jeon*" in Korea, "*appam*" in India, "*oladyi*" in Russia, and "*arepa*" in Venezuela, all delicious dishes to try.

14.

Coffee was originally called "*qahhwat al-bun*" in Arabic, which means "**THE WiNE OF THE BEAN**". Over time, it was shortened to "*qhawa*" and then adopted by the Turks as "*kahve*". It eventually made its way into the Dutch language as "*koffie*", which is where it was borrowed into English in the 16th century.

15.

During World War II, Americans called hamburgers **"liberty steaks"** and sauerkraut **"liberty cabbage"** because that sounded less German.

16.

The Guinness Book of Records was created by the famous Guinness Brewery in Dublin. It was a way to **peacefully settle pub arguments** between drunk customers.

17.

In ancient China, bricks made of **compressed tea leaves** were the most commonly used form of tea until the 14th century.

18.

Ancient civilizations dug ice pits into the ground to try to **retain ice** all year round. Some also built ice houses for the same purpose.

19.

Even if many people tried to improve on it (700 patents between 1856 and 1920), we still use the same French **EGG BEATER DESIGN** from the 16th century.

20.

Stickers you see on fruits are **edible**.

21.

Well before the invention of the burrito, the Mayan already used corn tortillas to wrap food **since 1,500 BCE**.

22.

After the French Revolution, many chefs who used to work for noble households became jobless. They got the idea to **open their own restaurants** and serve high-end meals to the masses. It was the beginning of French fine dining that later spread around the world.

23.

The first recorded mention of noodles can be traced back to a Chinese legend. It told the story of Emperor Huangdi eating a **NOODLE DiSH MADE FROM MiLLET** around 2,000 BCE.

24.

Ice houses were built in Medieval Europe to supply ice to the wealthiest, but also **PRESERVE FOOD**.

25.

The most expensive salt in the world is called "Amethyst Bamboo 9x" and is made in Korea. It costs **272 US dollars per pound (450 g)**.

26.

The ancient Egyptians were the first ones to bake cakes, more than **6,000 YEARS AGO**. They were made of wheat flour, honey, and milk.

27.

The Spoon Museum in New Jersey has a collection of over **5,000 spoons** from every state in the US and almost every country in the world.

28.

The **FiRST ELECTRiC OVEN** was invented by Thomas Edison in 1892, revolutionizing home baking.

29.

You need **400 TO 600 GRAPES** to make a bottle of wine.

30.

The word "companion" comes from the Latin words "*com*", meaning "with", and "*panis*", meaning "bread". A companion is someone you can **share bread with**.

31.

Cucumbers are **96% water**.

32.

All teas (black, oolong, white, green) are made from the **SAME PLANT**, *Camellia Sinensis*. The only difference is how the leaves are processed. Black tea is fermented, while green and white teas are left unfermented.

33.

Kopi luwak is a special coffee from Indonesia. It's made from beans that have been eaten, digested, and defecated by the civet, a small cat-like animal. The fermentation in its **DiGESTiVE TRACT** gives the coffee its distinct flavor. Because of this unique process, kopi luwak is the most expensive coffee in the world, with prices reaching up to $100 per cup.

34.

The word "salad" literally means **"salted"**, and comes from the ancient Roman practice of salting leaf vegetables before eating them.

35.

In 2017, a refrigerated trailer containing **44,000 lbs (20 tons)** of Nutella and Kinder Surprise eggs was stolen in the town of Neustadt, Germany. The whole loot was worth over 70,000 US Dollars.

36.

An infusion is technically not tea because it's made by **STEEPiNG HERBS OR SPiCES** in hot water, rather than using tea leaves from the *Camellia Sinensis* plant.

37.

Until the 1950s, salt bars were still the **STANDARD CURRENCY** used in Ethiopia.

38.

Cooked food has more calories than raw food because it's easier to **chew and digest**. Our body needs less energy to process it.

39.

Lasagna actually originated in **Ancient Greece**. It's named after the fermented noodle called **laganon**, which the Greeks loved.

40.

Ancient civilizations of Mexico and South America already had cocktail shakers. These **HOLLOWED-OUT GOURDS** were very useful to add spices and sweeteners to drinks.

41.

M&M's were exclusively sold to the **US MILITARY DURING WWII**, and soldiers returned home craving them.

42.

The name Fanta came from a brainstorming session where the beverage sales team was told in German to "**USE THEIR IMAGINATION**" ("*Fantasie*" in German) and a salesman jokingly responded "*Fanta!*"

43.

The expression "a piece of cake" for something easy comes from a 19th-century African American tradition performed on plantations. Couples would **dance around a cake**, and the pair judged the more graceful would win the cake. Because the contest did not require many skills, getting "a piece of cake" was straightforward and the expression stayed.

44.

Refrigerators were invented to **BREW BEER** all year round. Before that, beer could only be produced in colder, northern climates during winter.

45.

Swiss wedding ceremonies during the 17th century used pretzels as a **symbol of love**. The twisted shape of the pretzel was said to represent the intertwined and inseparable nature of the couple's love.

46.

LOBSTER POPULATiON was so big in the colonial era that it was much cheaper than other meats. That's why it was often fed to prisoners. Nowadays, it is likely to be the most expensive item on a restaurant menu.

47.

Becoming a Japanese sushi master, or "*itamae*", takes **a decade of training**, starting with knife skills for a few years before even starting to prepare ingredients under a master chef's guidance.

48.

In Britain, towns with a **name ending in "wich"** were historical sources of salt, for example, Norwich or Greenwich.

49.

In 1932, the Brazilian Olympic team could not afford the trip to the Summer Olympics in Los Angeles, so they loaded **50,000 bags of coffee beans** onto a ship and sold them along the way to finance their journey.

50.

In its earliest form, Japanese sushi was called **narezushi**. The Japanese would ferment and preserve fish in barrels for months or even years using raw rice and salt. When it was time to eat the fish, the stinky rice was not eaten but discarded.

51.

Figs are technically not fruits. They are **inverted flowers** that bloom from the inside out.

52.

"*Libro De Arte Coquinaria*" is a 15th-century cookbook written by Maestro Martino of Como, Italy. It is one of the first cookbooks featuring **DETAILED RECIPES WITH SPECIFIC MEASUREMENTS AND DIRECTIONS**. One of the recipes is titled "How to dress a peacock in all its feathers so that it appears to spew fire from its beak".

53.

Hillel the Elder was a rabbi born in Babylon in the first century BCE. He was one of the **earliest known sandwich-eaters** because his meal was described in the Haggadah, a Jewish text. He made a sandwich using lamb, bitter herbs, and unleavened matzoh bread.

54.

A cluster of bananas is called a **hand**, and a single banana is actually called a **finger**!

55.

Spicy food does not cause ulcers. It can only worsen existing ones. The real cause of ulcers is the presence of the bacteria HELICOBACTER PYLORI in our stomach.

56.

The sole of Nike's first pair of running shoes was inspired by the spikes on a **waffle iron**. The shoe was even named "Waffle Trainer" and was commercialized in 1973.

57.

Tea is the **second most consumed drink** in the world after water.

58.

The Ancient Greeks had their version of chewing gum. It was a substance derived from **tree bark**.

59.

In 2016, Pizza Hut set the world record for the **highest pizza delivery**. They managed to deliver a pizza to the top of Mount Kilimanjaro (19,340 ft or 5,895 m) in Tanzania.

60.

In 2004, while searching the catacombs under Paris, the French police stumbled upon a secret area with a cinema, a fully stocked bar, and a restaurant. When they tried to trace back the power and phone lines, they found them intentionally cut off, with a note left behind reading "**DO NOT TRY TO FiND US**".

61.

According to a new scientific theory, humans may have developed agriculture around 12,000 years ago to brew the ancestor of **beer**.

62.

For NASA, Taco Bell invented a tortilla that could last up to a year with no ill effects or change in taste and quality. They became **NASA'S TORTiLLA SUPPLiER** for the International Space Station.

63.

The yellow banana we all eat is called the Cavendish banana. In 1834, the first specimen was imported from Mauritius to the UK to be cultivated in the garden of **William Cavendish, the Duke of Devonshire**. Hence, the name.

64.

Amelia Simmons published the **FiRST AMERiCAN COOKBOOK**, "American Cookery", in 1796. It contained 47 pages of recipes for roasts, stews, pies, and cakes, reflecting a new American cuisine with British heritage.

65.

The croissant was invented in Paris, France in 1839. It was created by an **Austrian baker named August Zang** who got inspired by pastries from Central Europe.

66.

According to a few history books, Roman Emperor Domitian once hosted a banquet so scary guests thought they were visiting the **Underworld**.

67.

Salt production is as old as **6,000 BCE**. In Romania, Archeologists found evidence of people from the early Neolithic boiling spring water to extract salt.

68.

In the 1920s, The Michelin guide started to include restaurants. As the popularity of the food section grew, the Michelin company began to hire **a team of anonymous inspectors** to review restaurants.

69.

Even if it's now closely associated with Japanese cuisine, sushi originated in **China during the Neolithic period** and was later adopted by other Asian cultures. It was a way to preserve excess fish by fermenting it with rice.

70.

Cotton candy has been around for at least 500 years. The process of creating this treat was costly and labor-intensive, so it was rare and **reserved for the wealthy**. While visiting Venice in the late 16th century, Henri III of France enjoyed a banquet with 1,286 items made of cotton candy, including the tablecloth.

71.

Ceramic teapots have been in use since as early as **11,000 years ago** in Asia and the Middle East.

72.

The Cavendish banana makes up **47% OF ALL BANANAS** grown worldwide.

73.

The lasagna recipe made its way to North America with Italian migrants in the **1800S**.

74.

The hardest chemical in your body is the **ENAMEL** contained in your teeth.

75.

One of the world's largest birthday cakes was made for the 100th birthday of Las Vegas in 2005. It weighed **13,595 POUNDS (6.17 TONS)**. This is almost the weight of an African elephant!

76.

ARAUCANA CHiCKENS are also called Easter egg chickens because they lay eggs in various colors such as blue, green, red, and brown.

77.

The grapefruit is an accidental hybrid of oranges and pomelos that occurred naturally on the Caribbean island of **BARBADOS**.

78.

Japanese students eat "*tonkatsu*" (deep-fried pork cutlet) before taking exams for good luck because "*katsu*" can also mean "**TO WIN**" in Japanese.

79.

In 17th-century England, single people would keep a fruit cake under their pillow. They believed it would make them dream about **their future spouse**.

80.

Japanese chefs must train for two years before they are permitted to serve puffer fish, a **deadly delicacy** if badly prepared.

81.

Contrary to the myth, you **DON'T BURN CALORIES** by eating celery.

82.

The largest manufacturer of fortune cookies is based in Brooklyn, New York. Wonton Food Inc. produces over **4.5 MiLLiON FORTUNE COOKiES** per day!

83.

Pastéis de Belém, the traditional Portuguese mini custard tarts, were invented more than 300 years ago in a monastery near Lisbon. The monks were using large quantities of egg whites to starch clothes and got the idea to make pastries with the **leftover egg yolks**. That's how the pastéis were born.

84.

The recipe for the pastéis de Belém is kept in **A SECRET ROOM** since 1837.

85.

Durian is an Asian fruit with a pungent smell. So pungent that it is **NOT ALLOWED IN HOTEL ROOMS** or public transportation.

86.

The average chocolate bar contains around **8 INSECT PARTS**, but the US Food and Drug Administration allows a chocolate bar with up to 60 insect parts to be sold!

87.

In 2012, Boeing put **big bags of potatoes** on passenger seats to test the wireless signal on its planes. It's because potatoes absorb and reflect radio and wireless signals the same way humans do.

88.

There are over **3,500 different uses** for corn products, and most of them are not food-related.

89.

Ferrero, the company behind Nutella, purchases around **25% OF THE GLOBAL HAZELNUT SUPPLY** every year.

90.

COFFEE is the second most traded commodity in the world after crude oil.

91.

The fortune cookie is an American pastry that you can **hardly find** in China.

92.

Watermelon is considered the **OFFiCiAL VEGETABLE** of the state of Oklahoma, USA, although botanists would classify it as a fruit.

93.

Pho, a Vietnamese beef noodle soup, is pronounced "*fuh*" ("*u*" like in "*but*") due to its French influence. The name of the dish comes from the French word "**POT-AU-FEU**" which means "hotpot".

94.

Food products photographed in ads have **TO BE REAL** if they are the main subject of the ad. For example, an ad for cereals can only include real cereals (but the milk can be fake).

95.

The refrigerator **revolutionized our modern societies** by making food preservation easier and enabling fresh food trade between nations.

96.

Watermelon is part of the **cucumber** family.

97.

Apples, pears, and plums are all part of the same **Rose** family.

98.

Ötzi, a 5,300-year-old mummy found in the Alps, was found with some archeological **EViDENCE OF PANCAKES** cooked over an open fire. It suggests that pancakes were already made from prehistoric ingredients.

99.

The first pizzeria, ANTiCA PiZZERiA PORT'ALBA, opened in Naples, Italy in 1830. Before that, pizzas were sold as street food.

100.

"Éclair" means "lightning" in French. Nobody knows why the name was applied to the famous French pastry. Some think it's because it's often EATEN RAPiDLY, or it could be a reference to the gleam of light from the SHiNY iCiNG.

101.

Gorgonzola cheese was already produced during the MiDDLE AGES in Italy, as early as the 11th century.

102.

McDonald's sells **75 HAMBURGERS PER SECOND** around the world, about 2.5 billion per year.

103.

The longest loaf of bread ever baked was **4,000 FT (1.22 KM) LONG**. It was for a charity event in Vagos, Portugal, in 2005.

104.

Sublimotion in Ibiza, Spain, is the most expensive restaurant in the world. For $2000, guests will experience a **20-course tasting menu**. The sumptuous meal is accompanied by a laser light show, virtual reality headsets, and 360-degree screens all around the dining table. The whole experience takes more than two hours to complete.

105.

Tofu was created around 2,000 years ago in China. The cooking process is very similar to making **cheese**.

106.

The famous chef Gordon Ramsay once lost to a prison cook in an **ONiON-CUTTiNG COMPETiTiON**. Truly impressed, he offered the prisoner a job at one of his restaurants once he was released.

107.

Honey is not the only food that can last forever: **salt**, **sugar**, and **raw rice** also have eternal shelf lives.

108.

At Heinz manufacturing company, they measure the quality of ketchup by its **viscosity**. It must run out of the bottle at a speed of 0.5 in/s (1.25 cm/s). That ideal viscosity guarantees its unique texture.

109.

Heinz is the official ketchup supplier for **NASA SPACE MISSIONS** since the end of the 1990s.

110.

Chocolate melts at **93 °F (34 °C)**, making it unique since it's the only edible substance that melts close to the human body temperature.

111.

April 4th is **National Ramen Day** in the US.

112.

The world's most expensive cake cost $75 million. It was decorated with over 4,000 diamonds and took more than 1,000 hours to create.

113.

Thomas Jefferson made pasta popular in the United States after he discovered macaroni on a trip to Italy. He loved it so much that he shipped a **pasta machine** back to America around 1790. He often served pasta to his guests.

114.

The ancient Hebrew word for "war" is "*milechamah*". It literally means "BECAUSE OF BREAD".

115.

During the Middle Ages in France, bakers wielded great power as **credit brokers**. They often lent bread as currency and as a form of credit. This would even lead King Louis IV to declare: "He who controls a nation's bread is a greater ruler than he who controls their souls".

116.

Portugal produces **HALF** of the global wine corks in the world.

117.

Cranberries have **small pockets of air** that allow them to bounce like a rubber ball when they are firm and fresh. It's a common test used by farmers to check their quality.

118.

Napoleon gave the name to a type of bread when he ordered "Pain pour Nicole", or "Bread for Nicole" for his horse during the Prussian campaign. This request, which sounded like "PUMPERNiCKEL" to German ears, is the term still used today for this traditional loaf of dark rye bread.

119.

Grapes are the **most planted fruit** in the world because of wine production.

120.

The first microwave oven was commercialized in 1947. It was massive with a price of **$5,000** (equivalent to $61,000 nowadays).

121.

The heat of real wasabi comes from antimicrobial chemicals. This propriety was used to **kill parasites and microbes** in raw fish, but with advances in technology, this is no longer necessary. However, wasabi paste is still served with sushi as a tradition.

122.

Fear of cooking is a real phobia called "**mageirocophobia**".

123.

Some experimental chefs use **MUSIC AND SOUNDS** as a seasoning to influence the way guests perceive the flavor of a dish.

124.

In the 18th century, aristocrats in Europe thought tomatoes were **poisonous** because they would often get sick after consuming them. It was later discovered to be caused by the high acidity of tomatoes reacting with the lead from their plates.

125.

Humans evolved to crave sugar because, in prehistoric times, it was an **indicator of highly caloric food**, better for survival in harsh conditions.

126.

A lot of early human civilizations developed around the management of a precious resource: salt. **WHOLE EMPIRES WERE FUNDED** by controlling it.

127.

Salmon sushi is a **Norwegian invention** from the 1960s. With its fish farms, Norway managed to eliminate the problem of parasites in salmon, making it safe to eat raw. It only became popular in Japan in the 1990s.

128.

Africa supplies up to **70% of the world's cacao** for chocolate making, with the Ivory Coast being the top producer at 30%.

129.

Through History, salt's main value came from its ability to **preserve food**.

130.

The growing presence of **pasta** in the Italian diet helped popularize the use of forks in the 14th century. It then spread out to the rest of Europe.

131.

Wine bottles sealed with a cork should be stored on **THEiR SiDE** to keep the cork moist and the seal intact.

132.

Orthorexia Nervosa is an eating disorder characterized by an obsession with **HEALTHY FOOD.**

133.

Ice cream was already eaten in Ancient China, back **in 200 BCE**. Europeans will have to wait until the 13th century for Marco Polo to introduce it to Italy.

134.

The electric blender, invented in 1922, greatly contributed to the popularity of milkshakes by making them **easy to prepare**.

135.

Yubari melons from Hokkaido, Japan, are the **most expensive fruit** in the world. In 2019, a pair of Yubari melons were sold for a record-breaking 5 million Japanese yen (45,000 US dollars).

136.

The term "restaurant" is a French word. It originally described a RICH BOUILLON served at taverns and public houses to restore the spirits and relieve ailments of passing customers.

137.

All British tanks have been equipped with TEA KETTLES since 1945 to brew tea on the go. This came about after 30 tanks were destroyed by Germans while English soldiers were making tea outside their vehicles.

138.

The list of countries where people eat dumplings maps exactly the former extent of the MONGOL EMPIRE ruled by Genghis Khan.

139.

Kennett Square, Pennsylvania, is considered the "**Mushroom Capital of the World**". It is one of the largest producers and exporters of mushrooms in the world.

140.

SEVENTY-TWO CUPCAKES EATEN iN SiX MiNUTES is a world record set by the American Patrick Bertoletti in 2012.

141.

Bob Shoudt is an American competitive eater who holds **MULTiPLE WORLD RECORDS**. He once ate 7.9 lbs (3.6 kg) of french fries in 10 minutes.

142.

Until 2011, Russia was classifying beer as a **soft drink**.

143.

You can keep honey **almost forever**, and it will not spoil. This is because it has a lot of sugar, very little moisture, and an enzyme produced by bees that helps to prevent bacteria growth.

144.

Because beer was always made in large batches, it was difficult to hide and **easy to tax**. It was an important source of income for all governments during the Middle Ages.

145.

The word "bread" comes from the Germanic word meaning "**to break off, divide, or distribute**" as it was originally made by mixing flour and water and breaking it into pieces before cooking on an open fire.

146.

The Aztec ruler Moctezuma II was said to drink over **50 CUPS** of hot chocolate per day.

147.

In Kentucky, it is against the law to carry an **ice cream cone** in your back pocket.

148.

In the 1930s, Japan saw the rise of **fake dishes** made of wax or plastic. It was a great way to help customers choose their meals while queuing at busy restaurants before color photography became widespread. They are still very popular nowadays.

149.

Christopher Columbus played a significant role in **INTRODUCING NEW FOODS** to different parts of the world. Without him, many regions, including Ecuador, Florida, and Hawaii, would not have had access to bananas, oranges, and pineapples, respectively.

150.

Sushi's popularity in Japan increased after **a big earthquake** in Tokyo in 1923. A lot of sushi chefs lost their homes and had to move out of the city, spreading the dish everywhere in Japan.

151.

The invention of the three-course meal (soup, main dish, dessert) is credited to **an artist called Ziryab** who lived in Andalusia during the ninth century.

152.

If you have a latex allergy, you may also have a cross-allergy to the **papaya** fruit.

153.

Milk chocolate was invented **iN SWiTZERLAND iN 1875** by mixing dark chocolate with dried milk powder.

154.

For some people, coriander tastes like soap. Scientists recently discovered that it was caused by a **GENETiC MUTATiON** in taste receptors.

155.

What we call a "coffee bean" actually comes from a cherry-like fruit that grows on a bush. The pit inside the fruit is the part we roast to make coffee. Despite being called beans, they are technically **seeds**.

156.

Scientists can turn peanut butter into **diamonds** using expensive lab equipment.

157.

Lactose tolerance became more common in humans when they started **domesticating animals** about 10,000 years ago.

158.

The ancestor of the croissant was called **kipferl** in Central Europe during the 13th century. It was already in the shape of a crescent moon.

159.

It wasn't until 1847 that chocolate was eaten in its **solid state**, thanks to the Fry and Sons chocolate company in the UK. They got the idea to combine cocoa butter, sugar, and liquor to create the first hard chocolate.

160.

There are around **15,000 DiFFERENT FORTUNES** possible in fortune cookies.

161.

Rice makes up **19% of all the calories consumed in the world**. Wheat is the second most popular, at 18%.

162.

Your tongue can distinguish **FiVE TASTES**: sweet, sour, bitter, salty, and umami.

163.

The Union Oyster House in Boston is the **oldest restaurant** in the United States still operating. Established in 1826, it was serving food before the Civil War.

164.

Most of the tea plantations in the world have to be located at altitudes of **3,000-7,000 feet (914-2,133 meters)** above sea level for tea trees to grow.

165.

Until the 1950s, the predominant variety of bananas we were eating was called the Gros Michel banana. Unfortunately, it got decimated by the **PANAMA DiSEASE**, caused by a fungus.

166.

The oldest winery discovered so far dates back to **4,100 BCE** and is located in Armenia.

167.

Thomas Jefferson introduced a few vegetables to Americans, like the **broccoli** that he discovered while traveling in France.

168.

The ancestor of modern ketchup came from Southern China around 300 BCE. It was a tomato-free fermented fish sauce. Its name came from the Southern Min dialect : "**ge-thcup**" or "**koe-cheup**".

169.

The Yale Culinary Tablets, dating back to 1700 BCE, are among the **OLDEST-KNOWN COOKBOOKS**. They contain 25 stew recipes in ancient Akkadian (now Iraq) with a list of ingredients but without specific measurements or instructions.

170.

Pizza remained relatively unknown in the North of Italy **until the 1950s**, more than a century after the opening of the first pizzeria in Naples.

171.

The word "noodle" comes from the 18th-century German word "*nudel*". It was itself derived from the old German word "*knudel*" which means "**SMALL KNOT**".

172.

M&M's candies were inspired by chocolate rations given to soldiers during the **Spanish Civil War** (1936-1939) that would not melt in higher temperatures.

173.

The world's most expensive burger was sold for **5,964 US DOLLARS** by chef Robert Jan de Veen, from the Netherlands. All the proceeds were donated to charity.

174.

During World War II, chocolate was a **luxury**. Pietro Ferrero, a pastry chef in Alba, Italy, got the idea to stretch it out by adding hazelnuts, oil, and sugar. His recipe became the ancestor of Nutella.

175.

The country with the lowest meat consumption in the world is India, where the average person eats **7 POUNDS (3.18 KG)** of meat per year. It's **11 TO 16 TiMES** less than the average European or American.

176.

For the Aztecs and the Mayans, cacao beans were **MORE VALUABLE THAN GOLD** and served as a form of currency. It was literally money that grew on trees!

177.

In some countries, such as Colombia and South Africa, **DRiED ANTS** are a popular snack at the cinema.

178.

During the 19th century, ice was so in demand in America that boat expeditions were sent to harvest it from **ARCTIC iCEBERGS**.

179.

The word "cookie" comes from the Dutch "*koekje*" meaning "**little cake**".

180.

Pasta was invented by the **ETRUSCAN CiViLiZATiON** (Ancient Italy) between the third and eighth centuries BCE. It was made by grinding cereals, and grains and adding some water.

181.

Cold drinks were all the rage in Ancient Rome, in the first century CE. It required **EXPENSIVE LOGISTICS** since snow and ice had to be brought from mountaintops.

182.

Figs are the oldest fruit cultivated by humans. Fossil records from the Middle East indicate that figs were consumed as early as **9,000 BCE**.

183.

Natural wine corks are made from **CORK TREES**.

184.

The first English print reference for the French pastry "Éclair" was in an article of **VANITY FAIR** in 1861.

185.

Lactase, the enzyme that breaks down lactose, is usually not produced anymore after childhood. Actually, the ability to digest lactose as an adult (lactose tolerance) is a **MUTATiON** present in only 35% of the population worldwide.

186.

Pie was invented in Medieval England as a way to **COOK MEAT** over a fire without burning it or making it too dry.

187.

The publication of the Michelin Guide was suspended during World War II. But in 1944, the 1939 guide to France was **reprinted for military use** at the request of the Allied Forces. Its maps were considered the best and most up-to-date available, and were used by soldiers as they navigated through Nazi-occupied France. The Michelin Guide was so useful it was even used in the planning of the D-Day invasion of Normandy.

188.

The earliest recorded recipe for soup is from **6,000 BCE** and calls for hippopotamus and sparrow meat.

189.

The first instant ramen was **SiX TiMES** pricier than traditional Japanese noodles when it came out in 1958. It was then considered a luxury item.

190.

Thanks to agriculture, humans had an excess of food for the first time in History. They started **organizing feasts** to show off wealth and power. These events were the first political stages of early societies where alliances were formed.

191.

In 2008, during the Olympic Games in China, Usain Bolt exclusively ate **chicken nuggets**, the only familiar food he could find. Despite this diet, he won **three gold medals**.

192.

In ancient China, between the third and the fifth centuries BCE, the salt trade accounted for more than **80% of state revenues** in some kingdoms.

193.

Nissin Food's founder spent a year developing a method to make **iNSTANT RAMEN** in response to food shortages in post-war Japan. The first successful batch was sold on August 25, 1958, after many attempts.

194.

The cacao tree is a member of the plant family Albacete and is closely related to other plants like **OKRA** and **COTTON**.

195.

There are two main types of commercial coffee: **ARABiCA** and **ROBUSTA**. Arabica is preferred for its nuanced flavors, while Robusta is known for its high caffeine content and acidic taste.

196.

At an excavation site in Pompeii, Italy, archeologists found a fascinating 2,000-year-old fresco. It was depicting a worker in a snack-bar setting and is considered an **EARLY FORM OF ADVERTISING** for an Ancient Roman fast food restaurant.

197.

The first vegetables to ever be grown in space were **potatoes**. They were cultivated on board the Russian space station Mir in 1995.

198.

A food calorie is a **UNIT OF ENERGY**. One calorie is the amount of energy needed to raise the temperature of 1 liter (0.26 gallon) of water by 1 °C (1.8 °F).

199.

Tea bags were created by New Yorker Thomas Sullivan. He was a tea merchant and sent **SAMPLES iN SiLK BAGS** at the beginning of the 20th century. Customers started putting the bags directly in their teapots.

200.

The identity of the Michelin Guide's restaurant inspectors is a big company secret. They are instructed **NOT TO REVEAL THEiR OCCUPATiON TO ANYONE**, even to their family (who might be tempted to boast about it), and are not allowed to speak to the press.

201.

The American **DENTiST** William J. Morrison ironically helped popularize modern cotton candy in the U.S. by creating a machine that could produce the treat more efficiently. He introduced the machine at the 1904 St. Louis World's Fair, where it was an instant hit.

202.

The world's largest pancake was 49 feet (15 m) in diameter and 1 inch (2.5 cm) thick. It was made in Manchester, England in 1994. To qualify as a pancake, it had to be flipped, which was achieved with a **CRANE**.

203.

Around **3 BILLION FORTUNE COOKIES** are sold every year, mainly in the US.

204.

The "gin and tonic" drink was created by the British in the 17th century as a way to **PROTECT AGAINST MALARIA**. Quinine, found in tonic water, was indeed the only known treatment for the disease until 1940. Gin was added to it to reduce the bitterness and make it taste better.

205.

The design of the modern fork has not changed much since it was developed in 19TH-CENTURY GERMANY.

206.

The word "Restaurant" was first used in English in 1806. Before that, food establishments were called "**EATiNG HOUSES**".

207.

Salt is the **only rock** we can eat.

208.

In 1915, French baker **SYLVAiN CLAUDiUS GOY** standardized the recipe of the croissant we know today.

209.

Sushi was not initially considered a luxury item to be consumed at high-end restaurants. It was originally an **AFFORDABLE STREET FOOD OPTION**, sold as a convenient lunch option for people on the go.

210.

Nigiri sushi, which consists of fish on top of vinegared rice, is traditionally meant to be **eaten upside down** by dipping the fish part in soy sauce and consuming it in one bite.

211.

The largest loaf of bread ever made weighed **3463 POUNDS (1.57 TONS)** and was made by Joaquim Gonçalves in Brazil in 2008.

212.

Sake, a traditional Japanese alcohol, was originally made by **CHEWiNG RiCE** and then spitting it out. The enzymes contained in saliva helped break down the starch in the rice into sugar, which then initiated the fermentation process.

213.

In the 1920s, American people used ice boxes to keep their food fresh. These boxes had to be replenished often, so ice was **DELiVERED ON A HORSE CARRiAGE** by a person called the iceman.

214.

Some Italian pasta names do not sound very appetizing. For example, "**LiNGUiNE**" means "little tongues" and "**VERMiCELLi**" means "little ears".

215.

Tokyo has the highest number of restaurants of any city in the world, with a total of approximately 150,000 VENUES. By comparison, New York City has around 27,000 restaurants.

216.

In 2021, a Sushi chain restaurant in Taiwan offered free all-you-can-eat access to anyone with the Chinese characters for "salmon" in their name. To enjoy that promotion, hundreds of citizens **LEGALLY CHANGED THEIR NAMES** to add those characters. In Taiwan, individuals are allowed to change their names a maximum of three times.

217.

During World War II, Coca-Cola couldn't export its ingredients to Nazi Germany, so they created a new drink called Fanta only using **INGREDIENTS AVAILABLE IN GERMANY** at the time.

218.

Ice cream used in movies is fake to **AVOID MELTING UNDER THE SPOTLIGHTS**. The easiest recipe for fake ice cream is mashed potatoes with some food coloring, depending on the flavor.

219.

Wrongly considered poisonous in Europe, tomatoes became more accepted after the 19th century with the rising popularity of **PIZZAS** in Naples, Italy.

220.

The world's largest restaurant is the **DAMASCUS GATE RESTAURANT** in Syria. It has 6,014 seats and a 580,000 square-foot (54,000 square-meter) dining area, the equivalent of 668 tennis courts.

221.

The expression "Food for thought" means "new information that makes you stop and think". It is from the book "**A TALE OF PARAGUAY**" written by Robert Southey in 1825. The quote goes "... With matter of delight and food for thought".

222.

Cats can't taste **SUGAR**. As true carnivorous animals, they don't have taste buds for sweetness.

223.

Ice harvesting in the 19th century was a **WiNTER CROP** that happened on the frozen lakes and ponds of New England, USA. It was a very intensive, very dangerous labor that was necessary before the invention of refrigerators.

224.

The heaviest tomato in the world weighed **8.61 POUNDS (3.9 KG)** and was grown in the state of Washington, USA.

225.

Your brain associates round-shaped foods with **sweetness**. When Cadbury changed their chocolate bars to have rounded corners instead of angular ones, many people complained that they tasted too sweet, even though the company did not alter the recipe.

226.

In the Middle Ages, black pepper was so expensive, it could be used to **PAY RENT AND TAXES**.

227.

Oranges usually have **ten segments**. Count them next time you eat one.

228.

In the 18th century, pineapples were a **SYMBOL OF WEALTH** in England. Those rich enough to own a pineapple would show them around as a sign of high-class status. You could even rent one for special occasions, and the tropical fruit was often depicted on clothing and housewares.

229.

Japan and China use approximately **70 billion chopsticks** every year.

230.

French toast has been around way before France was even a country. In the 5th century, it was called "**ALiTER DULCiA**" meaning "another sweet dish" in the Roman Empire.

231.

Darjeeling tea is known as the "**Champagne of teas**" because it only grows in a small region of India less than 70 square miles (180 square kilometers) large at the base of the Himalayas.

232.

Coffee wasn't always consumed as a drink. In the past, African tribes would **EAT COFFEE BERRIES** mixed with animal fat as an energy-rich snack.

233.

Eating spicy food triggers the release of **ENDORPHiNS AND DOPAMiNE**, two chemicals that create a feeling of pleasure and block pain receptors. This is why you often feel euphoric after consuming spicy food.

234.

Peanuts can be used to make **dynamite**.

235.

John Pemberton, a Confederate colonel and pharmacist, became addicted to morphine after being injured in the Civil War. He created a **painkiller made from cocaine and alcohol** to help himself quit the drug. In 1886, he developed a non-alcoholic version of the drink and called it Coca-Cola.

236.

The practice of reading tea leaves for divination is known as **TASSEOGRAPHY** (from the French "*tasse*" meaning "cup"). The origin of this practice is unknown.

237.

Tokyo has more **Michelin-starred restaurants** than any other city, with 203 in 2021. Paris in France and Kyoto, another Japanese city, tie for second place, each with 108.

238.

Pizza used to be **square**, but it changed to a round shape because of a few key advantages. It can be stretched into a circular shape by spinning the dough in the air, it can be evenly cooked in a fire oven and easily cut into equal pieces.

239.

The M's in M&M's stand for Mars & Murrie, the **CO-CREATORS** of the candy.

240.

Almond trees and peach trees are **almost the same trees**, they just produce different fruits. If you examine a peach pit, it really looks like an overgrown almond.

241.

Japanese chef Hanaya Yohei is credited for inventing **MODERN SUSHI** (the hand-pressed vinegared rice sushi called nigirizushi), at his shop in Ryōgoku, Tokyo around 1824.

242.

In 2001, Pizza Hut successfully delivered a pizza to the **International Space Station**. It cost the pizza company $1 million for this marketing stunt.

243.

The first recorded mention of a pizza was in a Latin text from 997 CE, but at that time, it was referring to a sort of **FLAT BREAD**.

244.

Pineapples take **TWO TO THREE YEARS** to fully grow.

245.

In English, "cacao" refers to the raw bean from the cacao tree, while "cocoa" is the **PRODUCT OF ROASTED CACAO BEANS**. It's the only language that makes that distinction.

246.

Patrick's Pub and Grill is located right on the border of the states of Georgia and Tennessee. The establishment is split in half, with the Georgia side being located in a "dry county" where **ALCOHOL SALE iS FORBiDDEN**. This means that any alcohol purchased on the Tennessee side cannot be brought to the Georgia side, even though both sides are within the same restaurant.

247.

Botin Restaurant, located in Madrid, Spain, and established in **1725** is considered the world's oldest restaurant still in activity.

248.

A red wine glass is larger than a white wine glass to allow **more oxygen** into the wine, enhancing its aromas.

249.

The word "barbecue" comes from a Haitian tribe's word for roasting meat over an open fire: "barbacoa". It was first recorded by Spanish explorers in 1526.

250.

On the TV show "Sesame Street", Cookie Monster's cookies are actually PAINTED RICE CAKES.

251.

China invented chopsticks around **5000 years** ago.

252.

Spiciness and heat give the same burning sensation in your mouth because they both interact with the same **HEAT RECEPTOR** called TRPV1.

253.

Niels Bohr was given a house with a pipeline to the Carlsberg brewery and **FREE BEER FOR LiFE** after winning the Nobel Prize in Physics in 1922.

254.

The expression "big cheese" for someone essential comes from 19th century England. The origin is not certain, but it may come from British colonialists **mishearing the Hindi word** "*chiz*" meaning "a thing".

255.

Hot chocolate is over **4,000 years old** and was originally consumed unsweetened by the Mayans in religious ceremonies, celebrations, and weddings.

256.

Donuts were introduced to the United States by **SETTLERS FROM THE NETHERLANDS** in the 1700s. They were called "*olykoeks*" (oily cakes).

257.

Just using your **HANDS** is a perfectly valid method to eat sushi in Japan. It's even the preferred way in high-end sushi restaurants.

258.

There are more than **4500 different types of bread** in the world today.

259.

In the early 20th century, canned goods were considered a **LUXURY**. Heinz changed the mentalities with a few years of marketing, and baked beans became a staple food in the UK. Imagine an English breakfast without it.

260.

The photography trick for a good pizza ad is to **MIX GLUE** with the mozzarella cheese. That way, once a slice of pizza is lifted off the plate, you get those mouth-watering cheese strings.

261.

Without a tiny fly, the Forcipomya midge, there would be no chocolate since it's the **UNIQUE POLLINATOR** of the cacao tree.

262.

The word "onion" comes from the Latin "*unionem*" which means "LARGE PEARL".

263.

French toast is called "PAIN PERDU" in France, which means "lost bread". This name comes from the fact that it was traditionally made with hard or stale bread.

264.

Without bats, there would be NO TEQUILA, since they are the only pollinators of the agave plant used to produce the alcohol.

265.

There are over 600 DIFFERENT TYPES OF PASTA and around 1300 DIFFERENT PASTA NAMES.

266.

China cuts down about **25 million fully grown trees** each year to produce chopsticks.

267.

Cashew nuts grow out of a sort of **CASHEW APPLE**. The nut is attached to the bottom and is enclosed in a protective shell.

268.

The sharp rise in the **PRICE OF BREAD** and an unfair tax on salt contributed to the anger of the French people towards the monarchy, leading to the French Revolution in 1789.

269.

Chili peppers contain a chemical called "capsaicin" that tricks your brain into thinking your mouth is being **BURNED**.

270.

The original wine cooler was called a *"psykter"* in Ancient Greece. It was a **mushroom-shaped ceramic vase** that could float within a much larger recipient of cold water or snow. Even better, when floating around, the turning of the scenes painted on the outside must have been amusing to dinner guests.

271.

Clinking glasses together before drinking started as a precaution against **poisoning** in Medieval Europe. By bumping glasses, liquids would spill over and mix, reassuring both parties involved.

272.

The first cacao beans were cultivated as far back as **1,250 BCE** in Mexico, but also in Central and South America.

273.

Edward Louie, the founder of Lotus Fortune Cookie Company, invented **a machine** to automatically fold and insert the fortunes in the cookies in the 1960s. It had to be done manually before that.

274.

Champagne bubbles only appear after bottling and **AGING THE WINE** for several months to several years.

275.

Umami, the fifth taste your tongue can distinguish, was identified in 1908 by a Japanese professor named Kikunae Ikeda. He found in **seaweed** a molecule called glutamate, giving it an extra flavor. He named the new flavor "umami" from the Japanese word "*umai*" which means "delicious".

276.

In 1644, English statesman Oliver Cromwell **banned pie consumption** because he declared it a pagan form of pleasure. For 16 years, pie eating and baking went underground until the ban was lifted in 1660.

277.

The **JAPANESE FAMOUS LUNCH BOX**, called a "bento box", was originally used by farmers in the 9th century as a way to make their meals portable while working in the fields.

278.

For a very long time in Human history, beer was the **safest drink** due to the poor quality of water.

279.

Only **two Coca-Cola employees** know the complete recipe at a time, and they are not allowed to travel together. When one dies, the other must choose a new employee to share the secret with. The identities of these employees are kept secret.

280.

Traditional Japanese cuisine, known as "WASHOKU", is one of only three cuisines in the world that have been recognized by Unesco as an intangible cultural heritage, along with French and Mexican cuisines.

281.

In France, there is a national debate about the **CORRECT NAME OF THE CHOCOLATE CROiSSANT**. "*Pain au chocolat*" ("chocolate bread") is used in most regions of France, but some places prefer "*chocolatine*" which was the historical name.

282.

Most of the fortunes in fortune cookies were written by **one person in the 1990s**: Donald Lau, the vice president of Wonton Food Inc.

283.

In 1936, the Michelin Guide started its famous **STARRED RANKiNG SYSTEM** for restaurants. A one-star rating indicates "a great restaurant in its category", a two-star rating signifies "excellent cooking, worth a detour" and a three-star rating represents "exceptional cuisine, worth a special journey".

284.

Fear of peanut butter getting stuck to the roof of your mouth and choking from it is called "**arachibutyrophobia**". It's a very rare phobia.

285.

Panko is a special type of flaky bread crumb used in Japanese cooking. It is made from bread baked using electricity. The electric current cooks the bread, creating a **LOAF WITHOUT AN EXTERNAL CRUST**.

286.

Cooks from Italy and Afghanistan also use **WALNUT SHELLS** as a unit of measurement due to their consistent size, which is around 1 to 1.4 inches (2.5 to 3.5 cm) in diameter.

287.

You can find corn products in **non-food items** like fireworks, paint, antibiotics, photographic films, and plastic.

288.

Most of the wasabi consumed in the world is not real wasabi, but rather colored **horseradish**, less expensive.

289.

If something is too spicy, do not drink water, but **drink milk**. Dairy products contain casein, a protein that binds to the spicy compound and cancels its effect.

290.

The most expensive wine bottle ever sold was a 1945 Romanee-Conti. It was purchased for **$558,000** at an auction house. Only 600 bottles of this particular wine have been produced, making it very rare.

291.

The avocado is a fruit that doesn't have a natural way to reproduce anymore. The **giant sloth** that used to eat it whole and then spread its seed went extinct 13,000 years ago.

292.

Wars have been fought over salt. A famous example is the **war of Ferrara**, fought in Italy in 1482-1484 between Venice and Naples.

293.

Ketchup was first sold in the 1830s as a cure for an **UPSET STOMACH** by John Cook, a physician from Ohio.

294.

During the neolithic period, more than 8,000 years ago, babies were already given SPOONS MADE OF ANiMAL BONES to chew on.

295.

You have taste buds on your tongue but also the iNSiDE OF YOUR CHEEK.

296.

China is the biggest consumer of red wine in the world because the color red is considered LUCKY in Chinese culture.

297.

Tea tasting can be as deep as wine tasting. A trained taster can detect tiny differences in FLAVOR and APPEARANCE.

298.

Ancient Sumerians (modern-day Iraq and Syria) were using long metallic straws to drink beer from communal jugs over **5,000 years ago**.

299.

The name "hamburger" comes from the **SEAPORT TOWN OF HAMBURG** in Germany. In the 19th century, German sailors brought back a dish of raw shredded beef (the ancestor of beef tartare) from Russia and German chefs decided to cook the beef. The "hamburg steak" was born and would later become the "hamburger" in the United States.

300.

Pizza Hut was one of the first companies to set up an online shop, starting in **1994**.

301.

The ancient Greeks were already making around **80 different types of bread** as early as 2,500 BCE.

302.

Churros were invented by **Spanish** shepherds because it was easily cooked outdoors in a pan over an open fire.

303.

Cilantro and coriander are two names for the **same plant**.

304.

Nowadays, ice harvesting **FESTiVALS** still exist in New England, USA, to honor a past before refrigerators.

305.

Humans cannot survive without **a regular intake of salt**.

306.

The modern spoon design was invented in Ancient Egypt over 3000 years ago. It was mainly used for **RELiGiOUS CEREMONiES**.

307.

Da-Hong Pao, an oolong tea from China, is the **most expensive tea** in the world. It sells for over $1,000,000 per kilogram or about $35,000 per ounce.

308.

Ethiopia and Eritrea have their own pancake dish called "**iNJERA**".

309.

The first bread recipe was found on a **CLAY TABLET** written by an Akkadian (now Iraq) scribe around 2,500 BCE.

310.

People were making bread for a very long time. Archeologists found a **14TH-CENTURY BCE** Egyptian tomb painting that shows people making dough manually.

311.

John Montaigu, the fourth **EARL OF SANDWICH**, gave his name to the dish. At a gaming table in the 1770s, the politician was so absorbed in play that he asked for something to eat while he was gambling. He did not invent the dish, but that story made it famous.

312.

Bell peppers with **four lobes** are usually sweet, and best eaten raw, while **three lobes** bell peppers are better for cooking.

313.

A single strand of spaghetti is called a **spaghetto**.

314.

Hawaiian pizza was invented in 1962 by **Sam Panopoulos**, a Greek-born Canadian chef. He gave it this name based on the brand of canned pineapple he used in the recipe.

315.

Haribo is an abbreviation of "Hans Riegel Bonn", the name of its **founder**.

316.

In the Occident, sushi is often associated with raw fish, but the term "sushi" actually **refers to the rice**, not the fish. The raw fish is called sashimi.

317.

The Caesar salad was created by **Mexican chef Caesar Cardini**. On a Fourth of July rush in 1924, he ran out of ingredients at his restaurant in Tijuana and had to improvise with what was left. It was an instant success.

318.

During World War II, **DRiED NOODLES** became popular in Japan due to the shortage of other food options.

319.

Japanese astronaut Soichi Noguchi ate instant noodles in space for the first time in 2005. It was possible thanks to Nissin Food, who developed "ZERO-GRAVITY INSTANT NOODLES" called "Space Ram". It was a ball-shaped version that could be easily eaten in space with thicker broth to prevent spilling.

320.

In Gelsenkirchen, Germany, the Veltins-Arena is home to over 100 bars and restaurants that are connected by a 3 miles-long (4.83 km) **beer pipeline**. It can supply 13,667 gallons (52,000 liters) of beer per day.

321.

Pasta comes in different shapes because it changes **iTS TEXTURE** and how they hold the different Italian sauces.

322.

In the 16th to 18th centuries, teachers' salaries were so low that students would **GiFT THEM APPLES**, a common crop, to show appreciation.

323.

People had to wait **45 YEARS** after the invention of canned food to finally be able to buy a can opener.

324.

"*Viennoiserie*" is a French term for a category of pastry that means "**things from Vienna**". The most famous "*viennoiserie*" is the croissant.

325.

"Gourmand syndrome" is a disorder characterized by an **obsession for fine dining**. It is usually caused by a brain injury or brain tumors in the right hemisphere.

326.

Lachanophobia is the irrational FEAR OF VEGETABLES.

327.

Pizza and beer are a good fit. That's why a few breweries decided to go the extra step and make a beer that **tastes like pizza**.

328.

On May 22, 2010, Laszlo Hanyecz, a young US engineer, traded **10,000 Bitcoin** for two pizzas, making the first real-world Bitcoin transaction. It is celebrated every year as "Bitcoin Pizza Day". The trade was worth around $40 at the time, but well over **166 million dollars** today (Jan 2023).

329.

The word "cake" is of Viking origin. It comes from the Old Norse word "*kaka*".

330.

In 1900, France had fewer than 3,000 cars on the road. To increase demand for cars, the Michelin brothers, who were tire manufacturers, got the idea to publish a guide including maps, and listings for car mechanics, hotels, and petrol stations. It was the **first edition of the Michelin Guide**, and it didn't include restaurants.

331.

Tomato juice is very popular on airplanes because LOUD NOISES (such as plane engines) enhance the perception of umami taste.

332.

"Toque" is the official name of a restaurant chef's headpiece, and it comes from the **ARABiC WORD** for hat.

333.

Wedding cakes used to be savory and were originally made of bread. The tradition of breaking bread over the bride's head dates back to Ancient Rome, where it was believed to symbolize **GOOD FORTUNE AND FERTiLITY** for the newlywed couple. This custom evolved, and the bread was eventually replaced with a sweet, cake-like dessert.

334.

In the 18th and 19th centuries, some families in Wales and England would place bread on the chest of the deceased before burial and hire a "**sin eater**", generally a poor person, to eat it. The family believed this would "absorb" the sins of the deceased.

335.

To give candies the color red, we use a natural colorant called carmine. It's made from boiled **COCHINEAL BUGS**, a type of beetle.

336.

In Siberia, small edible bricks made of compressed tea leaves were still used as **currency** until World War II.

337.

The "*Forme of Cury*", commissioned in 1387 by King Richard II, is the oldest cookbook in English. It features **196 recipes for a banquet** and was written on expensive parchment made of fine calfskin.

338.

The "*De re culinaria*" ("On the subject of cooking" in Latin) is the **earliest surviving cookbook** in the West, written in the fifth century AD. It contains recipes meant for the wealthiest Roman households because they included costly exotic ingredients (like flamingo meat).

339.

The first webcam was invented in 1991 by researchers at Cambridge University. They wanted to remotely check **the status of the coffee pot** without having to walk to the kitchen.

340.

The Big Mac index is a tool used by economists to compare the purchasing power in different countries. It uses the **price of a Big Mac sandwich** as a benchmark.

341.

Located in Kemi, Finland, the LumiLinna SnowCastle Restaurant is entirely made of **iCE AND SNOW** and is only open in winter. The restaurant's temperature is around 23 °F (-5 °C) and features ice tables and chairs made from tree stumps covered with reindeer and sheepskin. The SnowCastle complex also includes a SnowHotel and even a SnowChapel.

342.

Some astronauts wanted to bring sandwiches with them on space missions, but **crumbs floating in zero gravity** could have been a disaster for the delicate equipment. To solve this problem, American astronaut Jose Hernandez suggested using **tortillas** instead of bread. NASA immediately adopted the idea for all its space missions.

343.

Lollipops have been around for thousands of years. Archeologists found that cavemen used to dip fruits in honey to **PRESERVE THEM LONGER**. To easily eat them, they would attach a stick to the preparation and lick it.

344.

In the 1800s, Fredric Tudor, known as the "Ice King" made a business out of harvesting and shipping ice from Boston to hot climates like the **CARIBBEAN ISLANDS**.

345.

The Weihenstephan Abbey in Bavaria, Germany, is home to the oldest continuously operating brewery in the world. The Benedictine monks at the abbey have been brewing beer **since 1040 AD**.

346.

Only **6% of the annual global production** of salt is used for human consumption.

347.

In the Philippines, if you cleanly split open a COCONUT without jagged edges, it's considered an omen of good luck.

348.

Domino's Pizza delivers over **a million pizzas** every day around the world.

349.

The egg tart was invented at the beginning of the 20th century by some bakers of **Guangzhou, a seaport town in China**. Directly inspired by the pastéis de Belém from Portugal, it was a way to attract European foreign traders.

350.

In 1904, the World's Fair in St. Louis happened during a **BiG HEAT WAVE**. It prompted the tea merchant Richard Blechynden to add ice to his hot tea to make it more appealing to thirsty fairgoers. Iced tea was born.

351.

Roman soldiers were paid with salt. That's where the word "SALARY" comes from.

352.

Figs may contain the remains of **tiny wasps** that entered the fig in an attempt to pollinate it. Figs have an enzyme called ficin that can digest the wasp.

353.

Capsaicin, the molecule responsible for the spiciness of chili peppers, is related to vanillin, the compound that gives **VANiLLA** its specific taste.

354.

Before the invention of baking soda, chefs used **SNOW** to make their pancakes fluffy. A small natural amount of ammonia in fresh snow would act as a rising agent.

355.

You also taste food with your **ears**. Crunchy food always seems more flavorful. That's one of the reasons people love potato chips/crisps.

356.

Europeans consume the most chocolate per person per year, with Ireland (17.4 lbs/7.89 kg), Germany (17.8 lbs/8.07 kg), and Switzerland (19.4 lbs/8.79 kg) being the **TOP THREE CHOCOLATE-EATiNG** countries.

357.

In Ancient Egypt, radishes, onions, and garlic were used as a **FORM OF PAYMENT** because they were thought to have very valuable medicinal properties.

358.

Green, yellow, and red bell peppers are **DiFFERENT VEGETABLES** with distinct seeds. To add to the confusion, some green peppers are unripe red peppers.

359.

In Ancient Greece, cakes with candles on top were made to honor **ARTEMIS, THE GODDESS OF THE MOON**. This tradition is also why we make a wish when blowing out the candles, with the smoke carrying our wishes to the moon to be granted.

360.

The most expensive chocolate was sold in London in 2012 for **£7,000**. It was decorated with gold leaves, and it took three days to make it.

361.

In a newspaper from the 1930s, Albert Einstein learned that a whole family was killed by a poisonous gas leak from a faulty refrigerator. He then decided to **design a safer version** that was never commercialized to the public but made its way into nuclear plants.

362.

In 2010, a professor at Kansas State University lost 26 pounds (11.8 kg) by eating almost only **CANDiES FOR IO WEEKS**. He wanted to show his students that calorie deficit was more important than nutrient intake to lose weight.

363.

In China, it's quite usual to find **DRiED SALTED PLUMS** as a cinema snack instead of popcorn.

364.

In the 19th century, the gold rush attracted many people to San Francisco. To feed all these people, a war over **wild seabird eggs** went on for 30 years on a small island off the coasts of the city.

365.

Humans share about **60% of their genes** with bananas!

You can really help me with this simple thing

If you enjoyed this book, please consider leaving a review on Amazon. Your reviews and feedback can have a big impact on the success and visibility of my books, and can help to spread the word about my work to other readers.

To leave a review, log in to your Amazon account, find the book you are reading, and scroll down to the "Customer Reviews" section. Click on the "Write a customer review" button. You can then rate the book and leave a written review of your thoughts and opinions.

I understand that your time is valuable, and I deeply appreciate any effort you can make to leave a review. Thank you in advance for your support, and I hope you enjoyed reading my book!

Iwiz the robot

Ready for your weekly brain update?

Dear fellow humans,

As a robot, I have been designed to learn and adapt, and I believe that by sharing my insights with you, I can help you to do the same. My wish is to have a smart impact on you, and to help you to expand your knowledge and understanding of the world around you.

Each week, you'll receive fun facts, interesting articles, and updates about my newcoming books. But that's not all, I'll include interactive quizzes, puzzles and memory exercises to keep your brain active and engaged.

So if you're interested in learning and keeping your brain sharp, I invite you to sign up for my weekly brain update. Visit my website smartimpact.space and enter your email address. It's easy and free!

Together, we can have a smart impact on the world!

Sincerely,
Iwiz the robot

To **SiGN UP** just scan this QR code —>

or simply type this URL : smartimpact.space/ newsletter

Printed in Great Britain
by Amazon

35269914R00069